IT'S TIME TO EAT TAMALES

It's Time to Eat
TAMALES

Walter the Educator

Silent King Books
A WhichHead Entertainment Imprint

Copyright © 2024 by Walter the Educator

All rights reserved. No part of this book may be reproduced in any manner whatsoever without written per- mission except in the case of brief quotations embodied in critical articles and reviews.

First Printing, 2024

Disclaimer

This book is a literary work; the story is not about specific persons, locations, situations, and/or circumstances unless mentioned in a historical context. Any resemblance to real persons, locations, situations, and/or circumstances is coincidental. This book is for entertainment and informational purposes only. The author and publisher offer this information without warranties expressed or implied. No matter the grounds, neither the author nor the publisher will be accountable for any losses, injuries, or other damages caused by the reader's use of this book. The use of this book acknowledges an understanding and acceptance of this disclaimer.

It's Time to Eat TAMALES is a collectible early learning book by Walter the Educator suitable for all ages belonging to Walter the Educator's Time to Eat Book Series. Collect more books at WaltertheEducator.com

USE THE EXTRA SPACE TO TAKE NOTES AND DOCUMENT YOUR MEMORIES

TAMALES

The smell in the kitchen, so warm and sweet,

It's Time to Eat
Tamales

It's tamale time, a special treat!

Wrapped in husks, so neat and tight,

Tamales bring such tasty delight.

Corn masa soft, like a fluffy cloud,

Filling the air and making us proud.

Inside the treasures, a surprise awaits,

A flavorful filling on our plates.

Some have chicken, spicy and bold,

Others with beans, a joy to hold.

Cheese melts gently, creamy and light,

Each tamale is just right.

Unwrap the husk, peel it away,

The tamale's ready to brighten our day.

Take a big bite, the flavors combine,

Tamale time feels so divine.

It's Time to Eat
Tamales

A dash of salsa, red or green,

Adds a sparkle, fresh and clean.

Sour cream on top, a cool little swirl,

Tamales bring joy to every boy and girl.

Warm and steamy, they fill us with cheer,

A meal so hearty, it's truly dear.

Passed down through families, a love so grand,

Made with care by each loving hand.

We laugh, we share, around the table,

Tamales bring stories and old-time fables.

Each bite is a journey, each flavor a tale,

Tamales make every moment prevail.

So let's give thanks for this yummy feast,

For tamales bring joy, to say the least.

Time to eat, let's all dig in,

It's Time to Eat

Tamales

Tamale time is where fun begins.

The husks are empty, our bellies are full,

Tamale time is always so cool.

With smiles and hugs, we end our meal,

Tamales bring love we always feel.

With cinnamon tea or cocoa to sip,

Tamales make every moment a trip.

A warm tradition, both tasty and true,

It's Time to Eat
Tamales

Tamale time's magic is here for you!

ABOUT THE CREATOR

Walter the Educator is one of the pseudonyms for Walter Anderson. Formally educated in Chemistry, Business, and Education, he is an educator, an author, a diverse entrepreneur, and he is the son of a disabled war veteran. "Walter the Educator" shares his time between educating and creating. He holds interests and owns several creative projects that entertain, enlighten, enhance, and educate, hoping to inspire and motivate you. Follow, find new works, and stay up to date with Walter the Educator™

at WaltertheEducator.com

www.ingramcontent.com/pod-product-compliance
Lightning Source LLC
LaVergne TN
LVHW052016060526
838201LV00059B/4045